Original title:
The Dream Weaver's Garden

Copyright © 2024 Creative Arts Management OÜ
All rights reserved.

Author: Dante Kingsley
ISBN HARDBACK: 978-9916-90-766-5
ISBN PAPERBACK: 978-9916-90-767-2

Shades that Weave the Night's Tapestry

In the quiet hush of dusk's embrace,
Stars begin their whispered chase.
Moons of silver glide in flight,
Painting shadows, soft and light.

Velvet drapes the world in dream,
Colors dance in a gentle beam.
Whispers cradle the silent trees,
As the night hums with secret pleas.

Beneath the sky's deep, endless sigh,
Phantom lights flicker and lie.
They beckon forth the thoughts anew,
In the woven hues of midnight blue.

With each breath, the cosmos sways,
Eternity sleeps in the night's array.
Embracing tales of love and lore,
In shades that weave forevermore.

Twilight Blooms of Enchantment

In the hush of dusk's embrace,
Petals whisper tales of grace,
Colors fade to soft decay,
Nighttime dances, dreams at play.

Stars awaken, soft and bright,
Guiding hearts through velvet night,
Moonlit secrets, shadows weave,
In this moment, we believe.

Dreams Entwined in Nature's Caress

Beneath the boughs where soft winds sing,
Dreams take flight on whispering wing,
Nature's lullaby, sweet and clear,
Surrounds the soul, draws it near.

Sunlight dapples through the trees,
Gentle whispers of the breeze,
In every bloom, a story told,
Of love and life, a heart of gold.

Echoes of a Dreamscape Sanctuary

In the stillness of the morn,
Echoes rise, old thoughts reborn,
Gentle tides of memory flow,
In this haven, peace we sow.

Clouds drift softly, shadows play,
In the light of breaking day,
Every sound, a tender chord,
In the silence, spirits soared.

Pathways Through a Spiral Meadow

Winding trails of emerald green,
Call to wanderers unseen,
Each step taken, worlds unfold,
Stories waiting to be told.

Butterflies dance on whispered breeze,
Nature's art, a sweet reprise,
In this spiral, hearts align,
Every journey feels divine.

Secrets in the Verdant Shadows

Whispers curl in emerald bends,
Nature's hush, where silence blends.
Leaves conceal the tales untold,
In the quiet, secrets unfold.

Moonlight weaves through ancient trees,
Starlit skies, a soothing breeze.
Roots entwined like stories spun,
In the shadows, all is one.

Grove of Fanciful Fragments

In a grove where dreams will sway,
Colors dance in bright display.
Petals float on whispered sighs,
Nature's art beneath the skies.

Fragments of a fleeting thought,
In this haven, joy is sought.
Moments linger, soft and sweet,
In this place, our hearts will meet.

Dance of the Petal-draped Dreams

Petals twirl in soft embrace,
Dreams arise in this sacred space.
With each flutter, hope ignites,
In the dance of starry nights.

Whispers float on fragrant air,
Promises linger everywhere.
In the twilight, magic gleams,
Lost within petal-draped dreams.

Echoes from the Celestial Glade

In the glade where echoes play,
Stars align in bright array.
Voices call from far away,
Guiding footsteps, night and day.

Moonlit paths invite the soul,
Each shadow tells a story whole.
In the stillness, wisdom waits,
Echoes dance through heaven's gates.

Secrets in the Silk Meadow

Whispers dance upon the breeze,
Sunlight weaves through tangled leaves.
Colors bloom in gentle hues,
While shadows hide forgotten clues.

Fluttering dreams on petals lie,
Underneath the vast blue sky.
Footprints lost in dewy grass,
Echoes of the moments past.

Silken threads of endless night,
Twinkling stars, a soft delight.
Nature hums a secret song,
In this place where hearts belong.

Fantasies Beneath Woven Canopies

Underneath the ancient trees,
Lies a world that stirs the breeze.
Dappled light like stardust falls,
Magic whispers through the halls.

Petals shimmer in the shade,
Every color brightly laid.
Dreamers drift on thoughts so wild,
In this kingdom, free and wild.

With each rustle, tales emerge,
Crisp and clear like twilight surge.
Fantasies take gentle flight,
Lost in realms of pure delight.

Garden of Ethereal Echoes

In the garden where voices play,
Echoing the dreams of day.
Flowers sing a soft refrain,
Carried on the sunlit plain.

Misty shadows join the dance,
Inviting hearts to take a chance.
Every blossom holds a tale,
In whispers sweet, they softly hail.

Breezes carry scents divine,
Every note a secret sign.
The echoes weave a tapestry,
Of time and space, a symphony.

Blossoms of Celestial Reverie

Stars cascade like petals bright,
Painting dreams across the night.
In this realm where wishes flow,
Blossoms bloom, their magic grows.

Luna's glow bathes all in light,
Guiding souls through tranquil night.
Every bud a hope renewed,
In silence, beauty is imbued.

Celestial whispers fill the air,
Life's sweet promise lingers there.
In reverie, we drift and sway,
With every blossom's soft ballet.

Garden of Time's Tender Delights

Whispers of petals in the early light,
Dancing shadows play, a gentle sight.
The brook hums softly, a lullaby's tone,
In this sacred space, we are never alone.

Crimson roses sway with a fragrant breeze,
Joyful laughter mingles with murmuring leaves.
Every moment captured, like dew on a stem,
In this cherished garden, life starts anew again.

Mirage of the Illuminated Meadow

In the glimmering dusk, where the twilight glows,
Fields of wildflowers, a dream that bestows.
Shimmers of silver dance in the air,
Transcendent beauty is found everywhere.

Butterflies flutter with delicate grace,
In this enchanting, ethereal space.
Each step taken, a story unfolds,
Whispers of magic in colors so bold.

Nectar of Enchanted Thoughts

Beneath the ancient tree, shadows intertwine,
Dreams are like honey, deliciously fine.
Moments of stillness, where deep wisdom flows,
A treasure of thoughts, the heart gently knows.

The hush of the evening, secrets are shared,
In this garden of musings, all spirits are bared.
Nature's sweet nectar enriches the mind,
In the silence of twilight, our souls are aligned.

Splendors in the Midnight Bloom

In the depths of the night, where mysteries lie,
Blossoms unfold 'neath the starlit sky.
Moonlight drapes gracefully on petals aglow,
In this midnight magic, the wonders bestow.

Fragrance of jasmine drifts through the air,
Melodies whispered, a secret to share.
Each bloom a symbol of love's sweet embrace,
In the silence of night, we find our true place.

Reveries Among the Ferns

In emerald shades the ferns do sway,
While whispers of the breeze at play.
A dream unfolds in nature's seam,
Where thoughts drift softly like a stream.

Each frond a tale, each leaf a wish,
In tranquil moments we cherish.
Lost in time, we find our place,
In reveries, a warm embrace.

Celestial Roots and Dreaming Trees

Beneath the stars, the roots intertwine,
In dreaming trees, lost thoughts align.
Their branches stretch toward the night,
Filling hearts with calm delight.

These giants hold the secrets deep,
In silence, ancient memories sleep.
With every rustle, each breath a plea,
Whispers float through the canopies.

The Hidden Path of Blossoming Nightmares

Dark shadows dance where flowers bloom,
In hidden paths, we face our gloom.
Yet from the thorns, a beauty grows,
With every step, the heart bestows.

Nightmares twist into dreams at dawn,
As fears dissolve, we journey on.
With courage path we firmly tread,
In tangled woods, no tears are shed.

Mists of Imagination's Arbor

In vision's mist, the world unspools,
Where dreams are woven, hearts like fools.
Each sigh a spark, each thought a light,
Illuminates the shadowed night.

The arbor stands in stillness wide,
Where fantasies and fears collide.
Through foggy trails, our spirits soar,
Embracing all that lies in store.

Echoes Through the Flowering Aisle

Whispers dance on floral breeze,
Petals flutter, hearts at ease.
Sunlight spills in golden threads,
Nature's song, where love is spread.

Every bloom tells tales of old,
Secrets in their colors bold.
Paths of dreams beneath the sky,
Underneath the breezes sigh.

Through the rows of vibrant hues,
Footsteps trace the morning dew.
Echoes call in gentle tones,
Among the blooms, we're never alone.

In this place where time stands still,
Nature's voice begins to thrill.
Aisles that stretch like endless streams,
Carrying our sweetest dreams.

Shimmering Fables in Flora

In the glade where sunlight gleams,
Flora weaves our whispered dreams.
Every petal holds a tale,
Sparkling bright, it will prevail.

The daisies nod with wise delight,
As shadows dance in soft twilight.
Fables told in colors bright,
Paint the world in pure delight.

Turn each leaf and pause awhile,
Lost in every gentle smile.
Nature's heartbeats softly chime,
Shimmering through the threads of time.

In this realm where stories blend,
Magic blooms that never end.
With every sigh, the air is thick,
With shimmering fables, nature's trick.

Parables Among the Lilies

The lilies rise with grace and poise,
Silent whispers, nature's voice.
Each petal cradles life's own lore,
Lessons learned on yonder shore.

Among the blooms, the stories grow,
Softly told to those who know.
Each fragrance carries sweet rebirth,
In this sacred place of earth.

Rippling waters softly gleam,
Reflections echo every dream.
Parables in every hue,
Invite the heart to see what's true.

In gentle arms of nature's fold,
Wisdom shared through ages old.
Here in quiet, souls unite,
In harmony, the world feels right.

Garden of Gossamer Wishes

In the garden, wishes take flight,
Caught like stars in the gentle night.
Gossamer dreams float on the air,
Delicate hopes, a treasure rare.

Each flower blooms with a silent plea,
Whispers of what is yet to be.
Petaled secrets soft as lace,
Hiding in this sacred space.

Through the boughs of fragrant trees,
Life's desires drift like a breeze.
With every sigh, new dreams descend,
In this garden, all hearts mend.

Gossamer wishes, soft and light,
Dancing on the edge of night.
Nature cradles every wish,
In a world that learns to cherish.

Honeyed Hues of the Imagination

In the morning's soft embrace,
Colors dance and swirl with grace.
Golden rays on petals lie,
Whispers of a dream nearby.

Clouds hang low, a canvas wide,
Where thoughts like gentle breezes glide.
Every shade, a story told,
A tapestry of dreams untold.

Through the meadows, sunlight weaves,
A magic where the heart believes.
Courage blooms in every hue,
Painting visions pure and true.

With honeyed whispers in the air,
Imaginations soar and dare.
Each moment bright, a gem to find,
In the gallery of the mind.

Labyrinth of Illustrious Dreams

Wanderer, in a maze so deep,
Where shadows play and secrets seep.
Glimmers of hope shine through the dark,
Illuminating each hidden arc.

Footsteps echo on cobblestone,
Paths entwined like vines have grown.
Chasing echoes of lost desires,
Finding solace in silent fires.

Every turn reveals a choice,
Soft whispers call, inviting voice.
Into the heart of night we creep,
Within the dreams, we dare to leap.

In this labyrinth, truth may hide,
Yet treasures bloom where fears reside.
With every pulse, the moment gleams,
Embrace the maze of glorious dreams.

Serenade of the Wildflower Heart

Beneath the sky, a symphony,
Wildflowers dance in harmony.
With petals bright and scents so sweet,
They sing of love, where hearts do meet.

In fields alive with vibrant hues,
They sway softly, kissed by dews.
Nature's lullaby in the breeze,
A melody that never frees.

Each blossom tells a tale of grace,
A gentle touch, a warm embrace.
In wildflower hearts, dreams take flight,
Guided by the softest light.

So let us wander, hand in hand,
Through the serenade of this land.
With every bloom, a promise starts,
In the garden of wildflower hearts.

Sunlit Whimsy and Moonlit Quiet

In the sunlit hours, laughter flies,
Carefree moments, beneath bright skies.
Whimsical tales on the breeze,
Dancing shadows, a heart at ease.

As day gives way to twilight's glow,
The world transforms, a gentle flow.
Whispers linger as stars ignite,
In the embrace of moonlit night.

Softly weaving dreams so still,
In silence, the heart begins to fill.
With every twinkling light above,
The quiet speaks of endless love.

From sunlit whimsy to moon's delight,
Life's sweet serenade shines bright.
In joy and peace, we find our way,
Through the dance of night and day.

Petals That Paint the Sky

Petals dance on the breeze,
Whispers of colors so bright.
They swirl through the sun's warmth,
Filling the day with delight.

Underneath the vast blue,
Hearts bloom like flowers anew.
Every hue tells a story,
Of love's timeless glory.

As twilight paints its canvas,
Stars emerge with a sigh.
Petals drift towards slumber,
While dreams begin to fly.

In the hush of the night,
Hope lingers in soft sighs.
With each petal that falls,
A wish is born to rise.

The Forgotten Orchard of Echoes

In the heart of whispered trees,
Secrets linger in the air.
Fruits hang low, untouched,
Time forgotten, laid bare.

Echoes of laughter linger,
Carried on the gentle breeze.
The memories of summer,
Dancing among the leaves.

Old trunks tell tales of days,
When joy was ripe and free.
In shadows, dreams still wander,
Seeking what used to be.

In twilight's tender glow,
The orchard begins to sigh.
A symphony of silence,
Beneath an endless sky.

Threads of Serenity

Woven through the quiet night,
Stars gleam with gentle grace.
Each thread a whispered promise,
In this vast, celestial space.

Moonbeams stitch the silken sky,
Bringing peace to the weary soul.
With every twinkle, a reminder,
We are part of the whole.

In the calm of still moments,
Time unfurls its delicate kind.
Tangles of worry, unraveled,
Leave only solace behind.

As dawn spills warmth and light,
The threads find their embrace.
In the tapestry of existence,
Serenity finds its place.

Blooming in the Realm of Dreams

In the realm where shadows play,
Fantasies whisper and sway.
Flowers bloom in soft twilight,
Painting the edges of night.

Each petal, a thought unspoken,
Carried on winds of desire.
Colors burst into existence,
A world fueled by heart's fire.

Over hills of silver mist,
Dreamers tread with softest feet.
In this land of endless wonder,
Magic and reality meet.

As dawn nudges the dreams,
They fade like a fleeting sigh.
Yet the seeds of hope linger,
In the hearts that still fly.

Spectrums of Soft Serenity

In twilight's gentle embrace,
Whispers of calm arise,
Colors weave in the sky,
As day softly bids goodbye.

Breezes hum a sweet song,
While shadows begin to play,
Nature's hush feels so right,
In the fading light of day.

Stars shimmer, soft and bright,
With dreams that softly bloom,
In the night's tender peace,
Filling hearts with warm hues.

Hold the moment so dear,
As the world starts to rest,
Find comfort in the still,
In the night's soft caress.

Secret Boughs of Thought

Beneath the ancient trees,
Ideas dance in the shade,
Whispered secrets of old,
In the stillness displayed.

Leaves flutter like whispers,
As thoughts drift on the breeze,
Hidden paths intertwine,
In the heart of the trees.

Branches cradle the mind,
Holding dreams softly tight,
Among the secret boughs,
Thoughts take their gentle flight.

Silence deepens the spell,
Where imagination grows,
In the woodland's embrace,
The knowledge nature knows.

Echoing Petals of Yesterday

In gardens where time sighs,
Petals fall with a grace,
Memories softly linger,
In this cherished space.

Echoes of laughter play,
Among roses in bloom,
Each color tells a tale,
In the sweet perfume.

Winds carry whispers near,
Of loves we held so dear,
In the garden of dreams,
Each petal holds a tear.

As twilight steals the day,
And shadows softly creep,
We gather all our joys,
In the silence, we keep.

Fantasia Among the Roses

In a world lush and bright,
Roses dance in full bloom,
Colors swirl like a dream,
Filling hearts with their tune.

Petals speak in soft tones,
A language sweet and rare,
With each graceful whisper,
Love floats in the air.

Dreamers wander the paths,
Lost in fragrant delight,
Each turn holds a treasure,
In this magical night.

As stars twinkle above,
In this fanciful scene,
Roses tell tales of love,
In a soft, gentle sheen.

Fragrant Whispers of Forgotten Dreams

In silence blooms a gentle thought,
Whispers of what time forgot.
A fragrance lingers in the air,
Soft echoes weave a tender prayer.

Shadows dance upon the ground,
In twilight's breath, lost dreams are found.
Petals fall from memory's tree,
Soft reminders of what used to be.

Through winding paths where secrets lie,
Underneath the velvet sky.
Each step a story left untold,
In fragrant whispers, memories unfold.

With every breeze, a sigh, a kiss,
The heart recalls forgotten bliss.
In gardens deep, where shadows gleam,
Life's essence held in faded dream.

Spiral of Hopeful Petals

Around and round, the petals sway,
In colors bright, they laugh and play.
Each fragile form, a tale inspired,
In the dance of hope, never tired.

A twirl of joy beneath the sun,
With every beat, the hearts are one.
Spiraling dreams take flight with grace,
Finding their place in time and space.

In gentle winds, their stories soar,
Resilient souls that seek for more.
Petals whisper secrets, sweet and light,
Embracing day, inviting night.

Join the dance, let worries cease,
In spiral steps, find your peace.
For every bloom that graces Earth,
Brings a message of rebirth.

Blossoms of the Nocturnal Sky

In midnight's grasp, the blossoms glow,
Beneath the stars, their beauty flows.
With silver light, they softly gleam,
Each petal holds a tender dream.

The moon above, a watchful friend,
Guides the night until the end.
In fragrant hues of deepened night,
Whispers linger, soft and slight.

A tapestry of shadowed grace,
Each flower finds its sacred place.
With every breeze, a tale they weave,
In the night's embrace, we believe.

So let the darkness hold you tight,
In blossoms bright, find endless light.
For in the stillness, there's a spark,
That blooms anew, igniting the dark.

Garden of Frayed Edges

In tangled paths where wild things grow,
Life's beauty blooms in a gentle tableau.
Frayed edges tell the stories vast,
Of moments cherished, shadows cast.

Each petal worn by time's embrace,
Holds memories of a softer place.
The garden speaks in colors bold,
In every crease, a tale unfolds.

Through cracks and tears, new life emerges,
From roots that weave and nature urges.
Frayed edges cradle, nurture, mend,
Embracing flaws that never end.

In this garden, hearts find rest,
Among the wild, we are our best.
With every breath, a new song starts,
In the garden of frayed edges, we find our hearts.

Nature's Lullaby for the Wandering Soul

In whispers soft, the forest sighs,
Beneath the stars, where silence flies.
A gentle breeze, a calming touch,
Embracing hearts that crave so much.

The moonlit path, a guiding light,
To wanderers lost in endless night.
Each leaf a tale, each brook a song,
Where weary dreams together throng.

The mountains hum a sacred tune,
As petals dance, beneath the moon.
With every breath, the wild unfolds,
A tender hush, as night beholds.

So lay your head 'neath branches wide,
In nature's arms, there is no tide.
The night will cradle all your fears,
With lullabies of ancient years.

Boughs of Dreams Yet to Unfold

Beneath the arch of ancient trees,
Where every rustle brings a sigh.
Young dreams hang low, like ripened fruit,
Awaiting hands to grasp and try.

Soft whispers float on gentle air,
As shadows weave a tender shawl.
Each bough a wish, each bark a prayer,
For resting hearts that yearn to call.

With every dawn, new visions wake,
In tender light of fragile morn.
The path is paved with choices made,
And every step, a new dream born.

So linger here beneath the leaves,
Let nature's pulse guide every tread.
For in this space, where stillness breathes,
Lie boughs of dreams waiting to spread.

Enigma of the Nightshade Blooms

In twilight's cloak, a secret stirs,
The nightshade blooms in shadows' keep.
With petals dark, and whispers soft,
They guard the dreams that take the leap.

A dance of shades, between the light,
Where hidden truths begin to show.
Each flower holds a magic deep,
An enigma locked, a tale to grow.

The garden breathes in silent awe,
As colors blend in muted grace.
The nightshade sings of what's unseen,
A riddle wrapped in soft embrace.

So wander through this mystic land,
Where secrets lie in fragrant gloom.
Embrace the beauty, take the chance,
And solve the enigma of nightshade's bloom.

Cradle of Glimmering Fantasies

In twilight's hush, where dreams take flight,
A cradle swings in starlit air.
With whispers soft and wishes bright,
It holds the hopes we long to share.

The gentle sway of silver light,
Lulls wandering hearts to close their eyes.
Each glimmer calls the soul to rise,
To realms where endless magic lies.

A tapestry of night unfolds,
With threads of dreams that softly blend.
In cozy folds, all fears rescind,
And every heart soon finds its mend.

So join the dance of fantasies,
In cradles spun from stardust bright.
For here we weave our sweetest dreams,
In the embrace of tranquil night.

Illusions Amongst the Blossoms

In gardens bright, the petals sway,
Whispers of truth, hidden away.
Colors blend in a dance of light,
Illusions linger, take to flight.

A breeze holds secrets, soft and sweet,
Where time and dreams tenderly meet.
A fleeting glance, a moment's tease,
Life's fragile art, like rustling leaves.

Beneath the blooms, shadows creep,
In silent vows, the world does sleep.
Echoes of laughter fill the air,
Yet behind the smiles, there's despair.

In every flower, a tale does hide,
Of hopes that soared, then gently died.
Amidst the splendor, we seek to find,
Truth wrapped in petals, love unconfined.

Radiant Echoes of Untold Dreams

Silent wishes dance on the breeze,
Unwritten stories, hearts at ease.
Stars weave patterns, bold and bright,
Whispers of dreams, igniting the night.

Each shadow holds an untold tale,
Lost in the mist, like a hidden sail.
Echoes flicker in the moon's soft glow,
Guiding the wanderers, spirits aglow.

In the quiet moments, magic blooms,
Radiant flashes, dispelling glooms.
Promises linger in the night air,
Against the quiet, none would dare.

Chasing reflections of what could be,
Untold desires, wild and free.
The heart beats softly, seeking the light,
In radiant echoes, dreams take flight.

Veil of Petals and Stardust

In twilight's hush, the petals fall,
A delicate whisper, nature's call.
Stardust weaves through the evening's veil,
Secrets of space in fragrant trails.

Under the arch of silver skies,
Dreams take shape as the daylight dies.
A hush descends, the world slows down,
In petal soft curtains, heavily worn.

Each sparkle twinkles, a wish to share,
With each gentle sigh, we send a prayer.
Veils of soft color, shall we embrace,
In starlit gardens, we find our place.

Moments linger in the dusky glow,
Wrapping our hearts in the magic flow.
Petals and stardust, a world anew,
In the depths of night, the universe true.

Starlit Pathways Through the Foliage

Through whispering leaves, the moon does glide,
Casting its glow, a silvery tide.
A pathway opens, inviting and wide,
Starlit adventures where dreams coincide.

In shadows deep, the magic unfolds,
Secrets of life in the dark are told.
Under the stars, with each careful step,
The heart finds solace, the soul adept.

Crickets echo in harmonious tune,
Nature's lullaby beneath the moon.
Soft rustles beckon, guiding the way,
Through starlit pathways, night turns to day.

With every moment, the journey transcends,
Each heartbeat entwines, all doubts unbend.
Breathless we wander, on this enchanted track,
Starlit pathways, no turning back.

Whispers Among Starlit Vines

In the night where shadows play,
Vines curl gently, swaying low.
Whispers dance like silver light,
Secrets born under moon's glow.

Stars flicker, a distant tune,
Nature's breath soft in the air.
Each leaf tells a whispered tale,
Of love and dreams that linger there.

Crickets chirp in harmony,
While the night wraps us so tight.
In this garden, we lose time,
Together swaying in the night.

Lost in whispers, hearts align,
Starlit vines our sacred place.
In the quiet, we find peace,
Embraced forever in their grace.

Lullabies in the Quiet Grove

Beneath the boughs where shadows rest,
A gentle breeze begins to sing.
Lullabies that soothe the soul,
Nature's arms, our sleepy king.

Fireflies twinkle, soft and near,
Guiding dreams with their warm light.
In the grove, we close our eyes,
Drifting slowly into night.

Soft whispers float on serenades,
Branches sway in sweet embrace.
All worries fade like morning dew,
In this still and sacred space.

Lullabies wrap us in peace,
Every note a calming balm.
In this grove, our hearts will rest,
Together here, we are so calm.

The Secret Orchard of Wishes

In a place where dreams take flight,
An orchard blooms with whispered thoughts.
Branches bend with heavy fruit,
Each one a wish that time begot.

Petals soft as silken sighs,
Colors dance in the warm sun's glow.
Each fruit holds a secret kept,
Stories of hearts we long to know.

Beneath the boughs, we share our dreams,
Voices blend with the soft winds.
In this space of quiet hope,
A chance for healing where love begins.

The orchard waits for hearts to come,
With open hands to gently pick.
Wishes made in the dappled light,
In this secret, we grow thick.

Enigma of the Midnight Flora

In the stillness of the night,
Midnight blooms in shades of blue.
A fragrant puzzle, soft and sweet,
Whispers secrets known to few.

Ghostly petals shimmer bright,
Underneath the watchful moon.
With every step, the shadows dance,
Enigmas pulse in nature's tune.

Lurking whispers fill the air,
Mysteries weave through every leaf.
In the garden of the unknown,
Beauty sways beyond belief.

Flora wrapped in mystic dreams,
Time slows down, we start to see.
In this night, all questions fade,
Finding peace just you and me.

Palette of Luminous Fancies

In twilight hues, dreams commence,
Soft whispers dance, a world immense.
Colors blend, fate intertwines,
In each stroke, the heart defines.

Glimmers gleam on orchard's shore,
Chasing light, we long for more.
Every shade a tale to tell,
In this haven, all is well.

Stars aligned in velvet skies,
With painted eye, we realize.
Each hue a memory to face,
Life's canvas, a warm embrace.

In the brush, a spirit sings,
Of lands where joy and love take wings.
Palette wide, our hopes advance,
In luminous fancies, we find our dance.

Flowers of a Lost Horizon

Petals drift on summer's breath,
Whispers of a tale of death.
Colors fade where shadows loom,
In the dusk, blooms find their doom.

Once they danced in radiant light,
Now they sigh in fading night.
Gentle fragrance, memories loom,
In the garden's soft, cool gloom.

Each flower tells of love once found,
In vanished shades, hearts unbound.
Time moves on, yet still they stand,
Ghosts of dreams in silent band.

Within this realm where echoes play,
Lost horizons fade away.
But in the dark, a spark remains,
A hope that courses through our veins.

Haven of Silken Petals

In gardens where the breezes sigh,
Silken petals blush and fly.
Cascades of colors, soft and bright,
A haven found in gentle light.

Whispers mingling in the air,
Nature's art beyond compare.
Every bloom a secret space,
Where time pauses, leaving grace.

Crimson dreams and azure skies,
In this realm, the spirit flies.
Waves of silk in hues divine,
A sanctuary, pure, benign.

Here, beneath the ancient trees,
Hearts awaken with the breeze.
In every petal, worlds unfold,
A haven cherished, bright and bold.

Romancing the Twilight Garden

In twilight's realm where shadows play,
Hearts entwined in soft array.
Petals whisper, secrets flow,
In this garden, love will grow.

Moonlight dances on the leaves,
Casting dreams as night deceives.
Stars above in tender gaze,
Wrap our souls in night's embrace.

Fragrant blooms, a sweet perfume,
In this magic, hearts consume.
Each soft sigh a love song sweet,
In the garden, spirits meet.

Romancing realms where echoes blend,
In twilight's arms, our hearts transcend.
Forever caught in night's cascade,
A twilight garden, love conveyed.

Threads of Fantasia

In a realm where dreams intertwine,
Colors spark and stars align.
Whispers dance on silken threads,
Awakening worlds where magic spreads.

Each beat of heart, a story told,
Adventures bright, and spirits bold.
Through the corridors of time we float,
Chasing echoes in a dreamer's boat.

The tapestry of life unfurls,
Painting visions of fantastical swirls.
With every thread a path is spun,
A journey endless, never done.

In shadows deep and morning light,
We weave our dreams, a wondrous sight.
Threads of fantasy, delicate and fine,
Bind our souls in a grand design.

Blossoms of Forgotten Whispers

In the garden where time stands still,
Blossoms bloom with fragrant thrill.
Whispers linger on petals bright,
Carrying tales of lost delight.

Each flower tells a secret fair,
Of laughter shared and tender care.
Bright colors brush the morning dew,
Painting memories both old and new.

Among the leaves, soft breezes sigh,
As forgotten dreams begin to fly.
A symphony of love's refrain,
Echoes gently in joy and pain.

These blossoms hold, in every hue,
The echoes of a life once true.
In their fragrance, the past reclaims,
The beauty of forgotten names.

Enchanted Petals Under Moonlight

Beneath the glow of a silvered night,
Petals shimmer with soft delight.
Moonbeams weave through blossoms rare,
Breathing magic into the air.

A dance of shadows, calm and sweet,
The world pauses in soft retreat.
In gardens where dreams take flight,
Enchanted whispers grace the night.

Each bloom unfolds a tale to share,
Of stolen moments, dreams laid bare.
Under the sky, hearts intertwine,
Bathed in the glow of the divine.

As stars blink down, a gentle calm,
Nature sings a timeless psalm.
Enchanted petals, a soft caress,
In the moonlight's embrace, we find our rest.

Tapestry of Twilight Blooms

In twilight's hush, blooms start to glow,
A tapestry woven, a gentle show.
Colors merge in a soft embrace,
Nature's palette, a sacred space.

Petals blush with the setting sun,
As day departs and night has begun.
Whispers of dusk dance in the breeze,
Telling secrets among the trees.

Each flower sings of the day gone by,
Under the watch of the evening sky.
A blanket of stars wraps the scene,
In the quiet, where dreams convene.

Together we share this tranquil view,
In the tapestry where night feels new.
With every bloom, a promise bright,
Of hope reborn in the soft twilight.

The Dreamscape of Wildflowers

In fields where colors dance with light,
Petals whisper tales of flight.
Breezes weave a gentle song,
In wildflower dreams where hearts belong.

A canvas brushed by nature's hand,
Each bloom a story, each scent a strand.
Here time stands still, the earth's embrace,
In this soft haven, we find our place.

Golden sunbeams softly gleam,
Every shadow tells a dream.
Beneath the sky, a vibrant sea,
In this wild world, we are free.

As twilight falls, the colors fade,
Yet in our hearts, the dreams are laid.
With memories of fragrant night,
We wander still in soft moonlight.

Fragments of a Shimmering Garden

In a garden where the sunlight plays,
Mirrors of dew catch morning's rays.
Each petal glows, a jeweled spark,
Whispers of beauty in the dark.

Fluttering wings grace the air,
While fragrant blooms hold secrets rare.
A tapestry of colors weaves,
In this haven, the spirit believes.

Tendrils reach for the azure skies,
Where echoes of laughter softly rise.
With every breeze, a memory stirs,
In fragile beauty, the heart endures.

As shadows lengthen, twilight sighs,
Magic lingers, and daylight flies.
Among the blossoms, dreams take flight,
In fragments of bliss, the world feels right.

Whispers of a Starlit Grove

In the grove where shadows play,
Stars above, they softly sway.
Moonlit paths, a silver thread,
Bringing peace where dreams are fed.

Whispers carry through the trees,
Songs of night, a gentle breeze.
Every rustle, a secret shared,
In the silence, we are bared.

Night blooms open, softly glow,
In this quiet, time moves slow.
Each twinkle, a promise made,
In starlit hues, our fears will fade.

Boundless wonder fills the air,
In this magic, hearts lay bare.
With every moment, dreams entwine,
In the grove, our souls align.

Tapestry of Celestial Blooms

In gardens lush, where galaxies bloom,
Colors burst, dispelling gloom.
Petals twinkle like distant stars,
In this realm, we heal our scars.

Threads of silver, whispers soft,
In the twilight, our spirits loft.
Each bloom a wish, a gentle sigh,
Underneath the velvet sky.

Wind carries tales of love and grace,
In this sacred, enchanted space.
Celestial dances, a cosmic song,
In the tapestry where we belong.

As the night wraps us in its cloak,
The language of flowers, softly spoke.
In every petal, a dream takes chance,
In this woven world, we find our dance.

Beneath the Canopy of Wishes

Beneath the trees, dreams softly sway,
Whispers of hopes greet the light of day.
Stars glimmer softly, like fireflies bright,
Cradled in branches, hidden from sight.

In the meadow, silence finds its song,
Gentle heartbeats where the souls belong.
Each leaf a promise, tender and true,
Beneath the canopy, wishes breakthrough.

Swaying softly in the evening breeze,
Lifted by laughter, the soul feels at ease.
Echoes of memories dance through the night,
In this sacred space, everything feels right.

With every sigh, the world falls away,
Time twists and turns as the shadows play.
Beneath the stars, our dreams intertwine,
In this tranquil space, love's endless line.

Threads of Nightfall in Bloom

As night descends, a tapestry weaves,
Handcrafted silk from the darkened eaves.
Stars twinkle softly, each thread aglow,
In gentle darkness, secrets unfold slow.

Moonlight drapes softly over the land,
Caressing the earth with its silver hand.
Petals unfurl in the hush of the night,
Revealing their beauty, kissed by soft light.

Whispers of shadows drift on the air,
Filling the stillness with mythical flair.
The midnight flowers sway, dance in delight,
Threads of a dream, woven through the night.

Lost in the magic of night's sweet embrace,
Each moment cherished, a sacred space.
The beauty of silence, a calming tune,
Threads of nightfall, soft as a June.

Enchanted Blossoms of the Mind

In the garden where thoughts come alive,
Enchanted blossoms in colors thrive.
Petals of dreams, unfurling to share,
Wonders of wisdom float softly in the air.

Each petal whispers of stories untold,
Adventures of hearts, both tender and bold.
The fragrance of wonder, sweet and divine,
Enlightened blooms, a true friend of time.

Under the sun, thoughts wander and play,
Chasing the shadows that dance on the way.
The mind's garden blooms with seeds of insight,
A beautiful palette, forever in sight.

In twilight's embrace, the echoes still chime,
In the heart's garden, blooms flourish in rhyme.
With every reflection, a new flower grows,
Enchanted blossoms, where the spirit flows.

Fantasies in Petal Form

Petals fall gently, dreams sprinkled like dew,
Fantasies bloom in an enchanting hue.
Whispers of hope drift through the green leaves,
Within each blossom, a magic believes.

In every color, a story unfolds,
Tales of adventures waiting to be told.
Lost in the fragrance, the spirit takes flight,
Fantasies woven in the heart of the night.

Each garden a canvas, designed by the sun,
Where wishes grow wild, and joy has begun.
Petals as pages, we turn them with care,
Fantasies linger in the sweet summer air.

With every new blossom, a wish takes its form,
Bathed in the sunlight, tender and warm.
In the world of the flowers, dreams always conform,
Fantasies flourish in petalform's storm.

Secrets in the Soft Glow

In twilight's hush, where shadows play,
Whispers linger, softly sway.
Beneath the stars, a secret keeps,
In gentle dreams, the heart now leaps.

Moonlight drapes the silent trees,
Carrying tales upon the breeze.
Echoes dance in quiet night,
Secrets shared in soft, faint light.

From embered glow, a spark ignites,
Hopes entwined in soaring flights.
In every ray, a story starts,
Softly weaving through our hearts.

Embrace the night, let shadows roam,
In the glow, we find our home.
Through flickers of that gentle ray,
Secrets blossom, fade away.

Harmonies of Haloed Blooms

In gardens rich with colors bright,
Petals sway in morning light.
Harmonies of nature's song,
In every blossom, we belong.

Each fragrant note, a story tells,
Of sunlit days and gentle wells.
Dancing bees in sweet delight,
Chasing shadows, taking flight.

A tapestry of woven grace,
In every bud, a warm embrace.
Together, they weave time's soft thread,
In whispered songs, where dreams are spread.

Beneath the sky, in vibrant hues,
The spirit dances, life renews.
In haloed blooms, our hearts unite,
Together basking in the light.

The Legend of Starlit Poppies

In fields of gold where silence dwells,
A legend stirs in whispered spells.
Starlit poppies, bright and bold,
Guard tales of love in petals told.

Each bloom a wish upon the breeze,
In moonlit nights, they sway with ease.
A dance of dreams, a flicker of fate,
Within these fields, we celebrate.

Beneath the stars, they softly gleam,
Echoes of an ancient dream.
In every petal, stories flow,
The legend lives where flowers grow.

With every sunset, shadows play,
In poppy fields, the past will stay.
A timeless dance of night and day,
In starlit whispers, hearts will stay.

A Dance of Color and Light

The morning sun breaks through the gray,
A dance of colors leads the way.
Crimson hues and gentle blue,
Brush the world in vibrant view.

With every step, the earth awakes,
In every breath, a magic quakes.
Beneath the sky, the shadows play,
In rhythmic beats, they sway and stay.

A symphony of light bestowed,
In every corner, life has flowed.
Dancing gently, day unfolds,
In weaving tales that time upholds.

And as the twilight softly glows,
The dance of color gently flows.
In night's embrace, we find our art,
With every pulse, we share our heart.

Threading Time with Delicate Flora

In gardens where the shadows play,
Fleeting moments drift away,
Petals whisper soft and low,
While time weaves threads that gently flow.

Each bloom a memory, bold and bright,
Captured softly in the light,
Their fragrance dances in the breeze,
Unlocking hearts with quiet ease.

Seasons turn, yet still they stay,
In hues of pink and bright array,
Nature's art in every form,
Reviving spirits, calm and warm.

With every glance, a tale unfolds,
Of ancient secrets, softly told,
Threading time with delicate care,
Flora's magic fills the air.

Serenading Silence in Shades of Green

In emerald depths where whispers dwell,
A symphony beyond the swell,
Leaves hum lullabies to the night,
Serenading shadows in soft light.

Mossy carpets cradle dreams,
While sunlight plays in silver beams,
Each rustling branch a gentle sigh,
Inviting peace, as time drifts by.

Calm embraces every breath,
In hues of life that challenge death,
Nature's quiet, soothing sound,
In greenest realms, true peace is found.

Serenading silence, hearts align,
In shades of green, pure and divine,
A tranquil world where spirits soar,
Awakening the soul to explore.

Realm of the Forgotten Petal

In twilight's grasp, a secret lies,
Where faded blooms meet starry skies,
Forgotten petals, lost in time,
In whispered echoes, soft and rhyme.

Among the ruins, they still bloom,
A testament to life's sweet loom,
Nature's blush in shades of gray,
Reminding us of yesterday.

Amidst the wild, they softly glow,
With stories only few may know,
A realm where memories intertwine,
In fragrant notes, a heart's design.

Though time may fade the brightest hue,
The essence lingers, fresh and new,
In dreams we find their beauty still,
In forgotten fields, our hearts fulfill.

Hallowed Grounds of Enchanted Visions

In hallowed grounds where wonders blend,
Enchanted visions never end,
Mystic tales in every stride,
Awakening the heart and mind.

Amidst the trees, a spell is cast,
Binding future, present, past,
Where whispers swirl in sacred air,
And dreams awaken, bold and rare.

Moonlit paths and starlit skies,
Reveal the truth behind the lies,
Each step unveils a hidden scene,
In realms where fate and time convene.

Hallowed grounds of timeless grace,
Reflecting light in every space,
With every heartbeat, visions gleam,
Enchanted worlds, a waking dream.

Songs of the Luminous Orchard

Beneath the moon's soft glow, they sing,
Whispers of fruits on every spring.
Petals dance with the evening breeze,
Nature's chorus puts the heart at ease.

Stars twinkle bright above their heads,
While crickets serenade the beds.
Each branch holds secrets, sweet and bold,
Stories whispered, silently told.

In twilight's embrace, the shadows play,
Cascading light at the end of day.
Ripened dreams hang, so close yet far,
Guided gently by a glowing star.

The orchard breathes in tranquil bliss,
Soft melodies fill the night's abyss.
Echoes linger as the dawn draws near,
Songs of the orchard, forever clear.

Murmurs from the Celestial Arboretum

In the heart of the woods, secrets lie,
Branches stretch beneath the sapphire sky.
Leaves are rustling in whispers deep,
Guarding the dreams that the cosmos keep.

Soft rays filter through the tangled green,
Painting a world that's rarely seen.
The breeze carries messages of old,
Tales of warmth, of courage, of gold.

Beneath the starlight, shadows entwine,
Every heartbeat, a sacred sign.
The limbs of trees reach for the divine,
Murmurs echo in a voice so fine.

In the arboretum's gentle dome,
Nature invites every soul to roam.
Here, within this sacred space,
Life's essence glimmers, a warm embrace.

Garden of Eternal Reveries

Step softly here where dreams are sown,
In the garden where the wild things roam.
Petals blush with the colors of thought,
Every corner holds what time forgot.

Fountains echo with laughter of days,
Each drop a memory that softly plays.
Sunlight bathes in a gentle glow,
Inviting the heart to rise and flow.

Roses speak in fragrant tones,
Tales of love and of ages flown.
Here, imagination takes to flight,
Whirling dances in the silver light.

In this haven, sorrow holds no sway,
Joy blooms forth in the light of day.
The garden whispers, weaving and bright,
Eternal reveries on the edge of night.

Mystical Flora of the Soul

In the depths of stillness, magic stirs,
Petals unfold like whispered flurs.
Each bloom a heart that longs to share,
Secrets woven in earthy prayer.

Vines that twist, embrace the air,
Swaying softly, without a care.
Colors merge in a vibrant dance,
Mystical flora takes a chance.

The essence of life flows rich and deep,
In fragile beauty, the soul finds sleep.
With every touch, a spark ignites,
Hidden wonders come to light.

Through gentle paths, the spirit roams,
Finding solace, a place called home.
In nature's arms, the soul is free,
Mystical flora, a symphony.

Whipped by the Breath of the Dusk

The wind whispers softly through the trees,
As the sun dips low and kisses the sea.
Colors blend as day starts to fade,
Nature's canvas, a twilight parade.

Birds settle in nests, their songs now hushed,
In the embrace of the night, the world is rushed.
Stars twinkle faintly, a shy, glowing show,
While shadows stretch long in the evening's glow.

The air carries scents of the closing day,
As dusk wraps the earth in a gentle sway.
Silent moments invite secrets to rise,
Bathed in the hush of the darkening skies.

Whipped by the breath of the dusk's gentle hand,
We find solace where silence can stand.
In the twilight's grip, our worries can cease,
As we surrender to the night's soft peace.

Hues of Life Amidst the Nightscape

A palette of colors adorning the night,
Deep blues and purples in soft, muted light.
Crickets sing tales of the day's sweet end,
While moonbeams dance, as if they transcend.

Dreams flare like lanterns in the cool evening air,
Each star a story, a spark, a prayer.
Leaves shimmer gently, reflecting the gleam,
Illuminating secrets held within a dream.

Amidst this splendor, whispers unite,
Painting the darkness with hope and delight.
In every corner, life settles and sighs,
As the heart fills with wonder beneath velvet skies.

Journeying through hues, we find our own place,
In the tapestry woven of night's warm embrace.
With each gentle breath, we feast on the sight,
Living in color, amidst the nightscape.

Shadows Under the Canary Canopy

Underneath the branches where whispers reside,
Shadows dance lightly, their secrets they hide.
Golden canaries flit through the leaves,
As twilight beckons, the mind gently weaves.

Sunlight retreats, surrendering its throne,
While silhouettes stretch like pale overstone.
Rustling leaves carry giggles from high,
As the world twirls softly under the sigh.

Murmurs of dreams float down from above,
While the heart finds a rhythm, a quiet love.
Softly the night wraps our worries in vines,
In the gentle embrace of a world so divine.

In shadows we gather, our spirits set free,
Underneath the canopy, just you and me.
We sway with the stillness, where moments do gleam,
In the heart of the night, we nurture our dream.

Whims of the Blossoming Night

As petals unfurl in the cool, damp air,
The night blossoms softly, with secrets to share.
Whims float about like soft velvet sighs,
Inviting the moon to illuminate skies.

Each flower a story, each scent a memory,
Drifting like whispers in a gentle reverie.
Winds carry laughter, a tender embrace,
In the rhythm of life, we find our own place.

Stars join the festivity, twinkling with grace,
As shadows play tag in the night's quiet space.
With dreams in our pockets, we dance beneath light,
Celebrating moments in the blossoming night.

Whims of the darkness, aflame with delight,
Awake the enchantments that drift in our sight.
Together we wander, in awe of the scene,
In the wonders bestowed by the night so serene.

Paradigm of Colorful Reveries

In a world of hues so bright,
Dreams take flight in pure delight.
Whispers dance on vibrant breeze,
Painting moments with such ease.

Crimson skies at dusk's embrace,
Golden fields, a tranquil space.
Emerald forests, magic found,
In every corner, joy unbound.

Endless shades in every glance,
Life's a vivid, endless dance.
With each heartbeat, colors blend,
This dreamscape shall never end.

The Hidden Bloom of Aspiration

Within the soil of thought's domain,
Seeds of hope begin to gain.
Beneath the surface, roots extend,
Silent struggles towards the end.

Petals shy, they start to rise,
Reaching softly for the skies.
Tangled dreams in gentle light,
In darkened corners, take their flight.

Nurtured by the tears we shed,
From every loss, they forge ahead.
In quiet spaces, aspirations bloom,
Illuminating every room.

Petals of Wonder in the Mind's Eye

Close your eyes, let visions flow,
In the mind's eye, wonders grow.
Delicate petals, soft and rare,
Each a secret, each a prayer.

Floating dreams like clouds of silk,
Sipping thoughts like honeyed milk.
Every moment whispers light,
Filling shadows, chasing night.

Carpets woven with the stars,
Journeying beyond our scars.
In the garden of the mind,
Endless beauty we shall find.

Wings Among the Blooming Shadows

In twilight's hush, the colors gleam,
Wings unfurl, a silent dream.
Among the blooms, the shadows play,
Dancing softly, night and day.

Whispers carried on the air,
Tales of wonder, free of care.
Fluttering hearts in gentle sway,
Finding magic on the way.

Each flutter speaks of love untold,
Stories woven, brave and bold.
In every shadow, light will find,
A kaleidoscope of the entwined.

Milton Keynes UK
Ingram Content Group UK Ltd.
UKHW020908291124
451807UK00013B/802